Stars & Planets

Published in Great Britain in MMXIV by
Book House, an imprint of
The Salariya Book Company Ltd
25 Marlborough Place, Brighton BN1 1UB
www.salariya.com
www.book-house.co.uk

PB ISBN-13: 978-1-909645-68-4

SALARIYA

1 3 5 7 9 8 6 4 2

A CIP catalogue record for this book is available
from the British Library.

Printed and bound in China.

Visit our website at **www.book-house.co.uk**
or go to **www.salariya.com** for **free** electronic versions of:
You Wouldn't Want to be an Egyptian Mummy!
You Wouldn't Want to be a Roman Gladiator!
You Wouldn't Want to be a Polar Explorer!
You Wouldn't Want to sail on a 19th-Century Whaling Ship!

Visit
www.salariya.com
for our online catalogue and **free**
interactive web books.

PAPER FROM
SUSTAINABLE
FORESTS

Stars&

Planets

Written by Margot Channing
Illustrated by Bill Donohoe
and Tony Townsend

CONTENTS

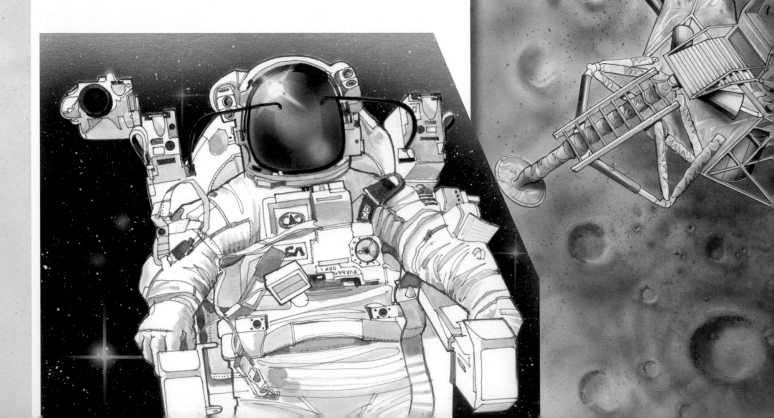

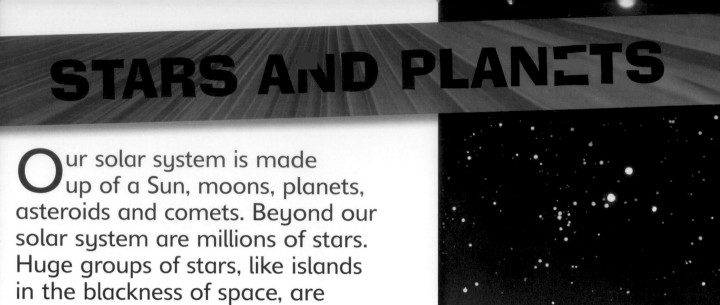

STARS AND PLANETS

Our solar system is made up of a Sun, moons, planets, asteroids and comets. Beyond our solar system are millions of stars. Huge groups of stars, like islands in the blackness of space, are galaxies. Galaxies, suns, moons and planets make up the universe.

TELESCOPIC EYE

Powerful telescopes allow us to see further into space than ever before. Hundreds of years ago, people knew the Sun only as a ball of light in the sky. Today, we know that the Sun is a huge ball of burning gas, many times bigger than our planet.

Sun

Space vehicles, such as space shuttles, have allowed us to travel into space to study its mysteries.

Moon

Earth

All of the planets in our solar system circle, or orbit, the Sun. Our moon is a natural satellite that orbits our planet, the Earth.

This book takes a closer look at stars and planets, from the Sun and all the amazing planets in our own solar system to the many billions of stars and planets that lie further out in the universe.

LOOKING OUT, LOOKING IN

Telescopes have shown us much of what we now know about the solar system and the stars beyond it. Telescopes magnify the light from distant stars and planets, showing that these specks of light are actually suns and worlds a little like our own.

SATELLITES IN SPACE

Human-made satellites orbit the Earth, sending pictures of our planet back to us. These images tell us much about the Earth's air, oceans, lands and cities. They show us what the weather will be like and help us to predict storms.

Storm

CROP FAILURES, CROP SUCCESS

Satellite pictures can help us to predict crop failures and famines in different parts of the world. Scientists use the images to decide which land is suitable for farming and which waters are rich in fish.

Satellites

Sahara Desert

From satellite information, scientists have a clearer picture of the Earth. They have seen that the Sahara Desert in Africa is spreading much more quickly than once thought. They also know that the Amazon Rainforest is not disappearing as quickly as they feared.

WORKING IN SPACE

High above the Earth, astronauts carry out experiments and other tasks that would be impossible on the ground. Powerful rockets send astronauts into space. By travelling high enough and fast enough, rockets escape the immense pull of gravity, which holds us on the Earth.

Flight deck

Space shuttle

SHUTTLE PROTECTION

There is no oxygen in space, so rockets carry an oxygen supply. This allows the astronauts to breathe. The space rocket also protects the human body from dangers, such as the deadly heat of the Sun and the freezing temperature of space.

Rocket

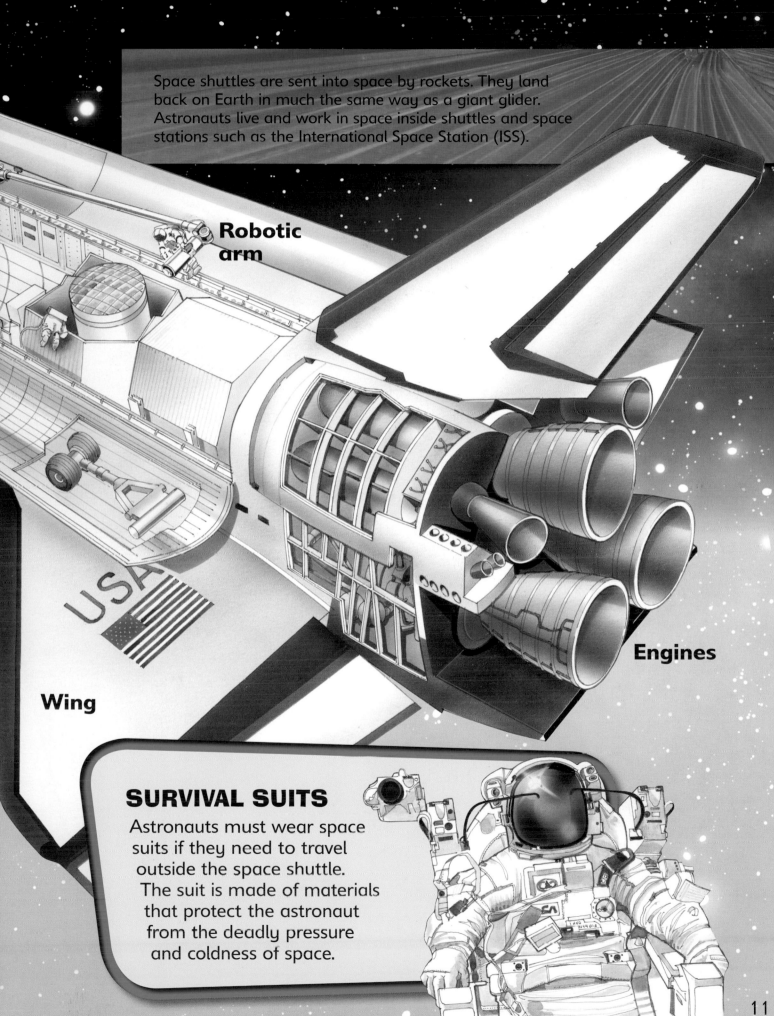

Space shuttles are sent into space by rockets. They land back on Earth in much the same way as a giant glider. Astronauts live and work in space inside shuttles and space stations such as the International Space Station (ISS).

Robotic arm

Engines

Wing

USA

SURVIVAL SUITS

Astronauts must wear space suits if they need to travel outside the space shuttle. The suit is made of materials that protect the astronaut from the deadly pressure and coldness of space.

THE MOON

Our nearest neighbour in space is the Moon. It is only one-quarter of the Earth's size. The Moon travels around the Earth, pulled by our planet's gravity. Nothing lives on the Moon – it is an environment without air or water. It would be impossible for life to survive there.

SURFACE OF THE MOON

The Moon has dark areas of lava that cooled and hardened 3,500 million years ago. It also has mountains and craters. One of the biggest craters is Clavius, which is 230 km wide and 3.6 km deep.

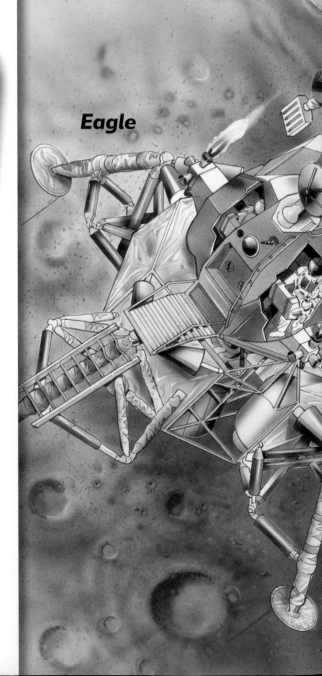

Eagle

Earth

Crater

Command module

MOON LANDING

In 1969, the US *Apollo* programme put the first astronauts on the Moon. 'Buzz' Aldrin and Neil Armstrong landed on the Moon in a module called *Eagle*.

Moon

The surface of the Moon is made of rock. Scientists believe that the Moon is formed of three layers – a crust 60 km deep, then a mantle 800 km thick, and a thick inner core.

VENUS AND MERCURY

Venus, Mercury, Mars and Earth are called the terrestrial, or 'Earth-like' planets. Venus is almost as big as the Earth, but Mercury is smaller. No other planets orbit as close to the Sun as Venus and Mercury. Sometimes, Mercury is just 46 million km away from the Sun.

Venus

VOLCANIC VENUS

Clouds full of sulphuric acid drop their deadly rainfall on Venus. The acid rain eats away at the planet's surface. Venus is extremely hot – even its coldest parts are like a hot oven!

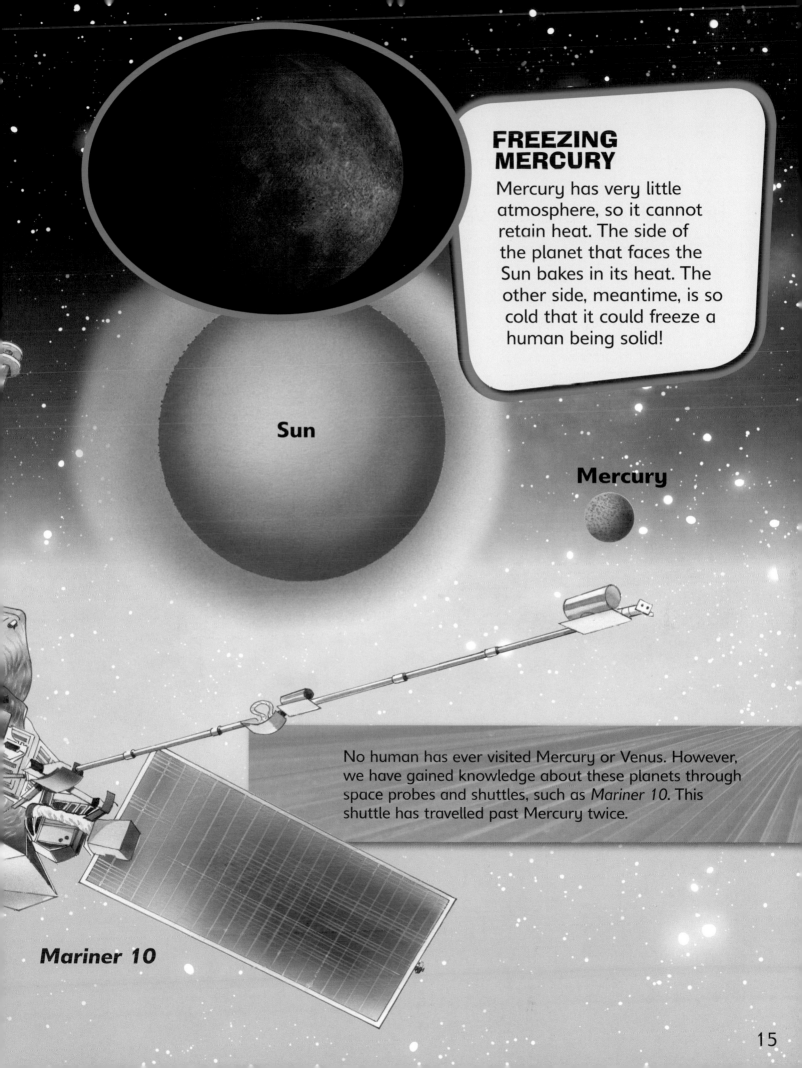

FREEZING MERCURY

Mercury has very little atmosphere, so it cannot retain heat. The side of the planet that faces the Sun bakes in its heat. The other side, meantime, is so cold that it could freeze a human being solid!

Sun

Mercury

No human has ever visited Mercury or Venus. However, we have gained knowledge about these planets through space probes and shuttles, such as *Mariner 10*. This shuttle has travelled past Mercury twice.

Mariner 10

MARS

Mars, the red planet, is named after the Roman god of war. Of all the planets, Mars's surface is most like the Earth's. Mars has rugged mountains, huge volcanoes, plains and deep valleys. Mars has an atmosphere, with clouds and winds that stir up dust storms.

LIFE ON MARS?

When the space probes *Viking 1* and *Viking 2* landed on Mars in 1976, they took photographs of its surface. These revealed many secrets about the planet, but they did not show any signs of life on Mars.

Viking Lander

LONG AGO

Mars has a very thin atmosphere, made up mainly of carbon dioxide. Humans could not breathe in this atmosphere. It is very cold and has many ice caps. However, millions of years ago Mars was much wetter and warmer than it is now. The planet's climate probably changed when meteorites crashed into it, stripping away much of its atmosphere.

Mars

Of the four terrestrial planets, Mars is furthest from the Sun. It is about 228 million km away.

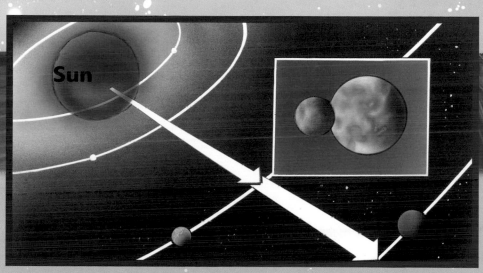

Sun

Earth

Mars

ASTEROIDS AND COMETS

A ring of rock and rubble called an asteroid belt orbits the Sun between the planets Mars and Jupiter. Its smallest pieces of rock are tiny dust particles; the largest are called asteroids. The largest of all is Ceres, which measures 920 km across. Thousands of asteroids travel through space.

HITTING THE EARTH

Most asteroids in our solar system travel between Mars and Jupiter. Some asteroids have come closer to the Earth, and some have even collided with it. Huge craters on the Earth's surface are the result of asteroids hitting our planet.

Asteroid hitting the Earth millions of years ago

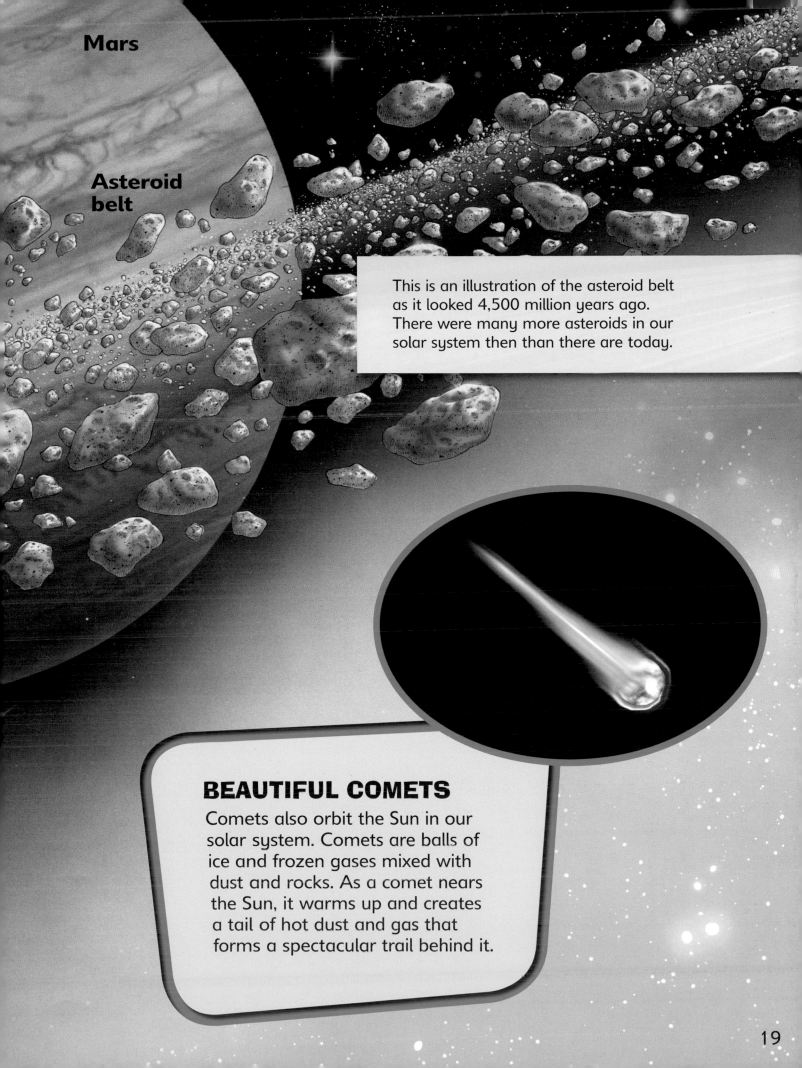

Mars

Asteroid belt

This is an illustration of the asteroid belt as it looked 4,500 million years ago. There were many more asteroids in our solar system then than there are today.

BEAUTIFUL COMETS

Comets also orbit the Sun in our solar system. Comets are balls of ice and frozen gases mixed with dust and rocks. As a comet nears the Sun, it warms up and creates a tail of hot dust and gas that forms a spectacular trail behind it.

THE OUTER PLANETS

Beyond the asteroid belt are four giant planets. Each one is named after an ancient Greek or Roman god. The first is Jupiter, then Saturn, Uranus and Neptune. After these comes the dwarf planet Pluto. The four giant planets are made of gas. Pluto is made of ice.

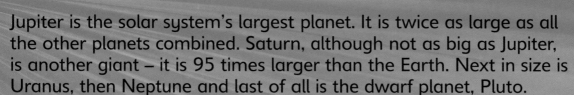

Jupiter is the solar system's largest planet. It is twice as large as all the other planets combined. Saturn, although not as big as Jupiter, is another giant – it is 95 times larger than the Earth. Next in size is Uranus, then Neptune and last of all is the dwarf planet, Pluto.

Jupiter

SMALLER THAN THE MOON!

The dwarf planet Pluto is almost 40 times further away from the Sun than the Earth is. It is the coldest, tiniest planet in the solar system. It is even smaller than the Moon!

Pluto

Neptune

Saturn

Uranus

JUPITER'S GIANT MOONS

Twenty-six moons orbit the planet Jupiter. Two of them, Ganymede and Io, are among the largest in the solar system. Ganymede is bigger than the planet Mercury, and Io is about the same size as the Earth.

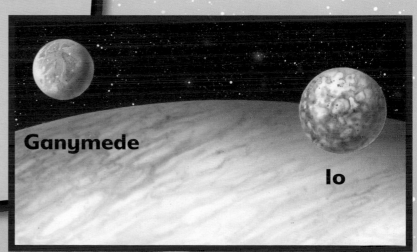

Ganymede

Io

THE SUN

At the centre of the solar system is its largest, heaviest, hottest and brightest object – the Sun. The Earth could fit inside this fiery ball of gas one million times. If you could weigh the solar system, the Sun would be more than 700 times heavier than all its moons and planets put together!

BURNING HOT

The temperature of the surface of the Sun is a sizzling 5,500 °C. Its centre, or core, is even hotter at 14,000,000 °C. Even 150 million km away on Earth, the Sun's heat can cause sunburn.

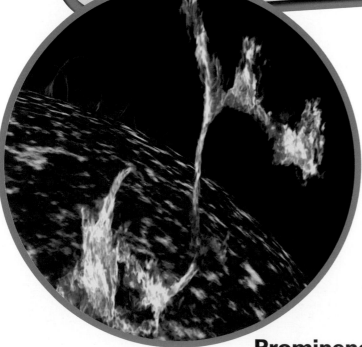

Prominence

Core of the Sun

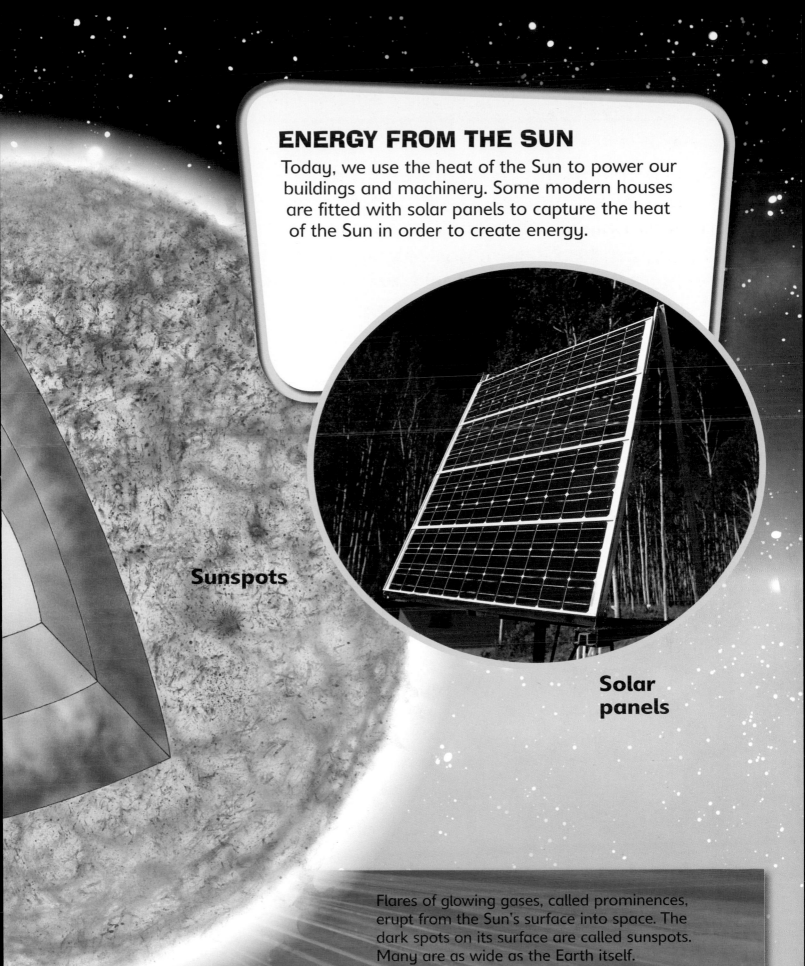

ENERGY FROM THE SUN

Today, we use the heat of the Sun to power our buildings and machinery. Some modern houses are fitted with solar panels to capture the heat of the Sun in order to create energy.

Sunspots

Solar panels

Flares of glowing gases, called prominences, erupt from the Sun's surface into space. The dark spots on its surface are called sunspots. Many are as wide as the Earth itself.

Prominence

On a clear night, you can see the tiny twinkling lights of several thousand stars. A telescope would reveal many more. Billions of stars shine deep in space. Stars are huge balls of gas. They look small only because they are so far away – some are as wide as Jupiter's orbit!

LIFE OF A STAR

No star lasts forever. Like people, they are born, grow and die. Stars begin as clouds of gas and dust called nebulae. Stars then grow into huge balls of gas. Eventually, stars use up all their gases and die.

Red giant

White dwarf

Black dwarf

DEATH OF OUR STAR

One day, the Sun will die. It will swell up and turn into a red giant that will swallow Mercury and kill all life on the Earth with its incredible heat. The Sun will then shrink to a white dwarf, no larger than the Earth. After that, it will cool into a black dwarf: a cold, dark, burnt-out ember.

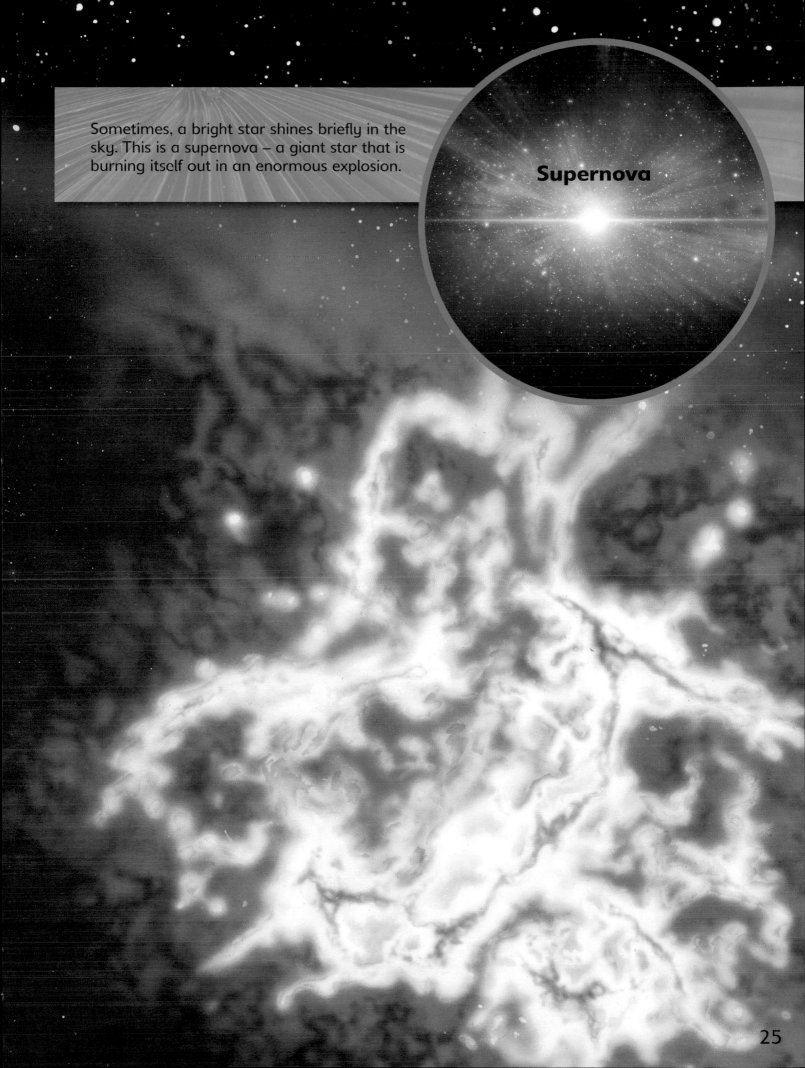

Sometimes, a bright star shines briefly in the sky. This is a supernova – a giant star that is burning itself out in an enormous explosion.

Supernova

STAR ISLANDS IN SPACE

If you gaze up at the night sky, you will see a milky-looking band of starlight. This is the Milky Way. It is made up of at least 100,000 million stars. These form the great system of stars that is our galaxy. The Sun and its planets are just one tiny part of the Milky Way.

HELD TOGETHER

The Milky Way is held together by the gravity of all the stars within it. If you could see the Milky Way from above, it would look like a giant pinwheel 100,000 light-years across.

Milky Way

OTHER GALAXIES

Beyond the Milky Way are other galaxies. Galaxies come in many different shapes. Some form spirals, like the Milky Way. Some are elliptical (oval), like a rugby ball.

Spiral galaxy

Elliptical galaxy

Irregular galaxy

Some scientists believe that a black hole lies at the middle of our galaxy. A black hole is a star that has died and collapsed to a pinpoint size. Its gravity is so strong that anything nearby will be pulled into it.

THE UNIVERSE

People have always questioned how the universe began. Scientists once believed that the universe, as we know it, had always been there. Others believed that it was once crammed into a space no bigger than a pinpoint before it exploded, scattering everything into space. Today, we know more than ever about the universe and how it began, but it still holds many secrets yet to be unlocked by scientists.

THE BIG BANG

Most astronomers now believe that 15,000 million years ago the Big Bang created space, time, energy and matter. From the size of a pea, the universe suddenly exploded into the size of the Sun. The universe then continued growing into the form we know it as today.

The Big Bang

COSMIC EXPLORATION

The Cosmic Background Explorer (COBE) satellite investigates background radiation that was created when the universe was born. In 1992, COBE showed parts of the universe becoming lumpy enough to form galaxies. This discovery has encouraged scientists to believe that the Big Bang theory is correct.

COBE

Scientists believe that our universe could change dramatically again in the future.

GLOSSARY

Asteroid a rock that orbits the Sun but is smaller than a planet.

Atmosphere the gases surrounding a star, a planet or a moon.

Black dwarf the small black ember of a completely burnt-out star.

Black hole a giant star that has collapsed into a dark, denser, tiny object. Black holes have a force of gravity so great that not even light can escape.

Comet a large object made up of ice, frozen gases, dust and rocks speeding around the Sun.

Gravity a force of attraction that tends to pull two objects together. Your weight is the force exerted on your body by the pull of the Earth's gravity.

Light-year the distance that light travels in one year (9,460,528,405,000 km).

Milky Way the galaxy that includes our own solar system.

Moon a mass made up of rock or ice that orbits a planet.

Nebula (*plural:* Nebulae) a cloud of gas and dust.

Orbit one object's path around another, like the Earth's path around the Sun.

Planet a large object orbiting a star, for instance, the Earth, which orbits the Sun.

Prominence a large flare of glowing gas that erupts from the Sun.

Red giant an aging star that swells up and turns from yellow to red as it begins to cool.

Rocket an engine that moves forward by thrusting burning gases backwards. Rocket engines work even in the emptiness of space.

Satellite a natural or artificial body orbiting a planet.

Solar system the Sun's family of planets, moons, asteroids and comets that orbit it.

Space probe an unmanned device that travels in space and sends back to the Earth information about other parts of the solar system.

Space shuttle a reusable type of manned spacecraft first developed in the United States.

Star a huge, very hot, bright ball of gas such as the Sun. Some stars are even bigger and hotter than our Sun, although very old stars tend to cool and shrink.

Sunspot a cooler, darker patch on the Sun's surface. Sunspots can last for hours or months.

Supernova a massive star collapsing in a giant explosion.

White dwarf a red giant or supergiant star that has cooled, faded and shrunk until it is no bigger than the Earth.

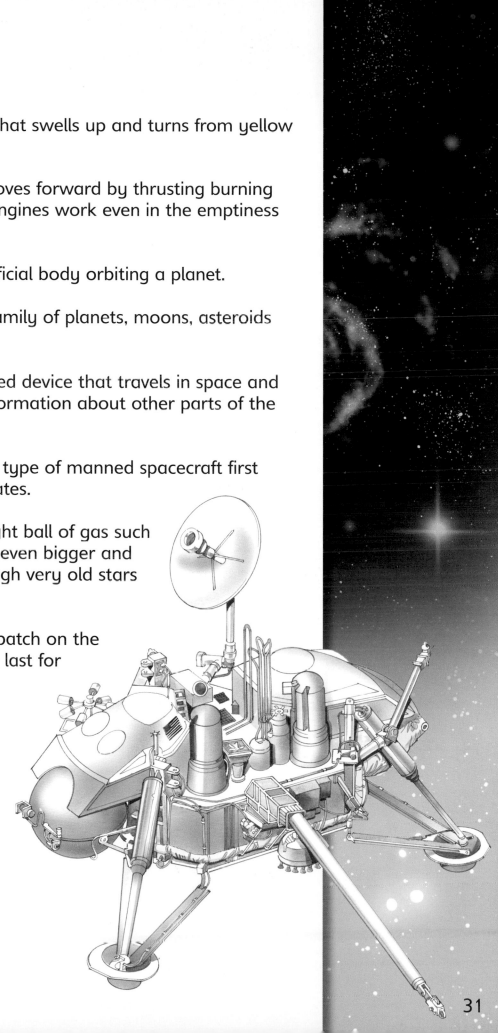

INDEX